BITCOIN

Copyright 2017 - All rights reserved.

You may not reproduce, duplicate or transmit the contents of this book without direct written permission from the author.

You cannot hereby under any circumstance blame the publisher. Nor may you hold him or her to legal responsibility for any reparation, compensations, or monetary loss owing to the information included herein, either directly or indirectly.

Legal Notice:
This book is copyright protected. This is only for personal use. You cannot sell, use, alter, distribute, quote, take excerpts or paraphrase in part or whole the content within this book without obtaining the consent of the author first.

Disclaimer Notice:
Please note the information contained in this document is for educational and entertainment purposes only. We have made every attempt to provide accurate, up to date and reliable information. We do not express or imply assurances of any kind. Readers admit that the author does not attempt to give legal, financial, medical or professional advice. The content of this book has come from various sources. Please consult a licensed professional before attempting any techniques outlined in this book.

By going through this document, the reader comes to an agreement that under no situation is the author answerable for any losses, direct or indirect, which they may incur because of the use of information contained in this article, including, but not restricted to, —mistakes, oversights, or inaccuracies.

BITCOIN

UNDERSTANDING BITCOIN

Charlie Pryce

https://www.amazon.com/dp/B078L85GTQ

Table of Contents

Introduction	1
Chapter One: The Virtual Currency	3
Chapter Two: Advantages and Disadvantages of Bitcoin	9
Chapter Three: Getting a Bitcoin Wallet	15
Chapter Four: Bitcoin Mining	19
Chapter Five: Making Money from Bitcoin	25
Conclusion	29
Resources	31

Introduction

Everyone wants to be part of the wave of change that is happening right now in the financial and technological industry. One of the current topics of interest is virtual money and cryptocurrencies. People want to do their transactions in seamless and straightforward ways. They want security and lower transaction costs. Others want to make a lot of money because the value of cryptocurrency units seems to appreciate every day.

There have been success stories about people who invested in Bitcoin and made huge amounts of money. People who bought Bitcoin when it was cheap and have watched it appreciate tremendously over the years are now rich. Whether you desire to make money, reduce transaction costs or find a secure way to make transactions, this book is for you.

In this book, "*Bitcoin: Understanding Bitcoin,*" you will learn what Bitcoin is, its advantages and disadvantages, how to make a Bitcoin wallet, how to trade Bitcoin, Bitcoin mining and the various ways that you can monetize this cryptocurrency. This book will help you get money so that you can begin to focus on what you want in life.

I will take you through the process of how this cryptocurrency works. I will do this by providing you with simple examples so that this information is palatable. There is so much buzz on Bitcoin right now, but before you even put your money into it, you need first to understand what it entails.

They say money is the root of all evil, but we cannot refute the fact that money makes life a bit more comfortable. Think about investing in Bitcoin, making a lot of passive income, and then having more time to spend with your loved ones while also chasing your dreams.

This book will cover everything you need to know about Bitcoin and getting started. After some time, you may want to delve deeper into cryptocurrencies if you plan to make it a career. This book is written as a guide for those who are just beginning to take interest in Bitcoin and want to understand what it's all about.

We will go step by step to ensure that you understand everything in detail. The ideal way to read this book is to go chapter by chapter. Do not move to the next section unless you have fully understood what the preceding chapter was about. This approach will help you absorb everything you are reading. You can take notes if you have to.

You may have heard the name Bitcoin floating around for a while now but never known how to begin. This is your chance to get started. Do not let this incredible opportunity pass you by. Grab this book and see what a difference this information makes!

Are you ready? Let's go!

Chapter One: The Virtual Currency

This chapter will share the history of Bitcoin and what cryptocurrencies are about. This approach is a great way to get your feet wet when it comes to this conversation. This chapter will be a reference point for other chapters in this book and cryptocurrencies as a whole.

Bitcoin History

Bitcoin came about as a concept when a programmer called Satoshi Nakamoto published a white paper about it in October 2008. It was just a concept, but people later adopted it because it was revolutionary. This idea came during the world recession that occurred around 2008. Satoshi then registered the domain name bitcoin.org and after that released the white paper so that people could understand what he envisioned.

In a nutshell, he wanted to make payments seamless and convenient. He tried to make a particular type of currency different from fiat currencies in the sense that people would trade with it online and one did not have to possess the physical asset as we do with paper money. However, this type of currency still possessed different qualities from fiat currency and these are decentralization, durability, divisibility, uniformity, scarcity, high quality, and portability.

The Idea

Satoshi wanted to create a calculation that has infinite possibilities. For example, in school, we learned that pi (22/7) is 3.14 and it can still be divisible to other decimal points that are infinite. Think about a mathematical calculation that has 21 million solutions. The person who gets the solution first will get some money, but it will be in a digital form. Since it is not easy for people to get that solution, this concept was the basis of how scarce Bitcoin would be. Just like real money, you have to work for it.

In the beginning, Bitcoin had no value, but when demand started to rise, more and more people began buying it. The fact that this digital coin was steadily gaining value made people start looking for it. As demand increased, more and more people began purchasing these virtual currencies. It is similar to how people value gold yet it is only a piece of metal. This is the same way that people have attached a value to Bitcoin.

This led to the creation of a market for Bitcoin where people could buy and sell it. When Satoshi registered his paper on Bitcoin, he kept it as an open source document so that everyone could read it and even study the code if they wanted to. This system ensured that other people could build upon it and make their additions and applications.

Although the system was free, there were still controls to ensure that all the users were on the same page. As of 1st December 2017, there were 16.7 million Bitcoin in circulation.

What is Bitcoin?

Bitcoin is a virtual currency, also known as "cryptocurrency." There are no physical notes or coins like there are with dollars. The cryptocurrency system is devoid of any administrative or government body controlling it. This is different from money because banks and financial institutions control the money supply. There is nobody that decides the amount of Bitcoin that will be in circulation. People create them by solving hard mathematical equations using their computers. They then trade them or hold them in store.

When it comes to cryptocurrency, transaction details are public information. People can see all the transactions because the peer-to-peer system is visible to everyone on the network.

Key Bitcoin Features

There are other cryptocurrencies like Litecoin and Etherium but they are all generated in their unique ways. You may be asking yourself how Bitcoin is different from other currencies and what makes it so unique.

Bitcoin has become so famous and valuable because it is the most common cryptocurrency and was one of the earliest. People talk about it and so the interest also grows.

Here are some key features of Bitcoin to note:

1. **Not tangible**: Bitcoin exists in a virtual space and you cannot touch it. However, you can see proof that it exists and you can trade it with other currencies. You can sell and buy it. You can see as it moves and you can keep track of the

transactions. You can trade it in for paper notes and coins.

2. **The system is decentralized**: Bitcoin operates on a peer-to-peer network where the entire Bitcoin community works together to keep the currency operational and secure. There is no governing body, and people can transact on the net without a third party.

3. **Not ubiquitous**: This means that not every place in the world has accepted Bitcoin. Today, you can go anywhere with USD and you can find a way to exchange it for the local currency. There is still much to be done when it comes to ensuring that Bitcoin is acceptable everywhere.

4. **Transactions are irreversible and take longer**: A Bitcoin transaction takes up to ten minutes to perform but once it is complete, it is irreversible. Therefore, ensure you know everything there is to know about Bitcoin and be sure when you do a transaction.

5. **Bitcoins are scarce**: They are not the same as standard currency. They do not have unlimited options like money. For example, when the money supply is less, the central bank can print more. Only 21 million Bitcoins will be in existence soon. The fact that they are limited means that the demand for them is very high.

With this background on the properties of Bitcoin, you may be asking yourself what makes it work and how it works. How do the transactions take place in the network? Here is some information that will help answer these questions:

1. **Transaction**: The deal represents the value from one person to another. You may do something online and get paid in Bitcoin. Just like money transaction, value and money move from one person to another. It is voluntary and two people have to agree to do the trade. Though it sounds simple, it is still possible for some people to forge or commit fraud on the system.

2. **Serial numbers**: Every transaction has a unique serial number to avoid forgery and theft. There is always a single public key, but there is also a private one too. A public key is what everyone on the network can see but a private key is a password to protect your funds. This option ensures that people have access to their resources and there are no duplicates for their transactions.

3. **What it means for banks**: The peer-to-peer network means that people can exchange money without banks being involved in any way. Today, for you to do a financial transaction with another person, there needs to be a bank or a third party to verify it, but with Bitcoin, there is no third party. Banks are scared that they will get phased out as people can now transact without them.

4. **Bitcoin mining**: This is one of the oldest ways of getting money through Bitcoin. However, it involves solving complicated math problems through a computer, and we will go into more details in Chapter 4. Mining is the process that creates the Bitcoin.

In this chapter, you have had a basic introduction to virtual currency and how Bitcoin works. We have also compared it to other cryptocurrencies and fiat money to see how it stacks up and what makes it so unique. With this information, you are well on your way to understanding different concepts in this book.

CHAPTER TWO:
ADVANTAGES AND DISADVANTAGES OF BITCOIN

At this point, you probably want to know what you are getting yourself into. This chapter will look at the advantages and disadvantages of Bitcoin. Like every new technology, this virtual currency has its good and bad side. Knowing this will help you decide if this is a viable venture or option for you.

Advantages

As mentioned in previous chapters, Bitcoin is a seamless method of payment. It has other desirable qualities that make it stand out. Here are some benefits:

1. **People are always improving the system**: It is a peer-to-peer technology where the network users are in control of the currency. There is the need for the Bitcoin software to be accessible to people so that they can communicate with each other on it. One of the advantages is that the users own the system and they have come up with ways to improve it and even build applications on it. Developers are always looking to make things easier for other users.

2. **Anonymity**: One of the most significant advantages is that it gives people privacy over their transactions. It is not the same as financial institutions which have traceable transactions. In

banks, anyone can get records of personal transactions. On the Bitcoin server, people can be anonymous because they use hash addresses. Unique *send* and *receive* addresses are generated during a transaction. These addresses change with each sale and it is hard for people to trace what one particular person is doing on the network. You can also make other transactions with Bitcoin anonymously because no central body keeps tabs on what people are doing.

3. **It is a great investment option**: The value of the Bitcoin has been increasing steadily over time. The idea is always to buy low and sell high in order to make your profit. However, you need to be very careful and to monitor its value.

4. **Interchangeability of Bitcoin with other cryptocurrencies**: Another advantage is that Bitcoin is very interchangeable and people can exchange it for other virtual currency.

5. **No transaction costs**: When you transact with the bank, you get charged a small amount that can become large when it accrues over time. There are no transaction costs in Bitcoin. However, in the future, there might be a transaction fee.

6. **No authority and taxes**: Today, when you buy something with your money or card, there is a tax associated with it. Currently, no government recognizes Bitcoin and therefore, there is no tax. However, when it becomes more widespread and accepted, there may be a tax.

Disadvantages

The fact that the currency is making a steady growth in popularity may be a good or a bad thing. There are many demerits and undesirable qualities of Bitcoin, including:

1. **Unpredictability**: In as much as the value of Bitcoin continues to surge, it is very hard to predict what will happen in coming years. There are proposers and opposers of Bitcoin and you can never be very sure. There have also been reports of an imminent crash to happen in the future. However, risk-lovers have invested in it knowing very well that the higher the risk, the higher the return.

2. **Security**: One disadvantage of Bitcoin is that it is possible for people to commit fraud on the system. People must be very wary of what applications they are using. Some past cases involved people losing their Bitcoin.

3. **Government interference**: This may not have happened yet but there are signs that administrative bodies want to clamp down on it and some even want to stop the growth of Bitcoin because it hurts their profits. The government in a country can decide that Bitcoin cannot be used in its banks. The truth is that governments and corporations are looking for ways to control it.

4. **Deflation**: There will be about 21 million Bitcoins in circulation in future but they are subject to deflation. There can be a recession if people hold on to their Bitcoin. When too many people hold on to the Bitcoin wanting the value to grow, there

might not be any Bitcoin left to make transactions with.

5. **Not convenient or easy**: Bitcoin is very complicated to use. You have to be tech savvy and you have to learn how to operate the different software so that you can do transactions. For fiat money, it is easy to go to the bank or use a credit card anytime. For Bitcoin, you have to be attentive and even get some help sometimes. However, ensure that you learn how to use it. Take as much time as you like to familiarize yourself with your software of choice. Many tutorials on YouTube will give you a visual on how to use these sites. If you are selling Bitcoin and getting money, do not release the Bitcoin until the other party has paid. The best advice is that you should always be paranoid. This will ensure that you have your security measures in check and you are not leaving anything to chance. However, over time, developers may make the software user-friendly and they can even get paid money for that.

6. **Not easy to understand**: Bitcoin is complicated, especially for the older generation. However, with some research and keeping up with the news, it becomes easy to understand.

7. **Skepticism**: There is a lot of skepticism when it comes to Bitcoin. It stems from the fact that not everyone understands it fully. Other people have their own theories on how Bitcoin is bad and is simply a scam. All this negativity may affect people from even investing in it.

8. **Not yet accepted**: Bitcoin has not yet been accepted as real money in some parts of the world.

There is no government that has backed it yet and once that happens, this will mean that it can be used anywhere just like USD is. People ascertain the value of the bitcoin and this keeps changing depending on the demand and supply. The virtual currency can also destabilize at any time. This can happen when people holding Bitcoin suddenly sell it and the panic can cause people to believe that it is not valuable.

9. **Theft**: There is no protection on the currency and you can actually lose it. You can easily lose your wallet if you are not careful. If you lose your Bitcoins, they will no longer be in the system. There is no guarantee that people cannot steal the Bitcoin and there is no way to reverse the transaction when that happens. This is a very risky affair.

10. **Used in Black Market**: The black market and dark web is where people conduct unscrupulous activities like paying for guns and financing crimes. The anonymity and privacy of Bitcoin enable people to use it for such transactions. This is a bad thing because it helps the spread of crime.

In this chapter, we have explored all the pros and cons of this cryptocurrency and you are better informed to decide if you want to invest in it or not. However, the fact that it is growing steadily in value and publicity may mean that it will all affect us in one way or another.

Chapter Three:
Getting a Bitcoin Wallet

This chapter will look at Bitcoin and how it works. We will also investigate how you can get a digital wallet. To get started with cryptocurrency, you must know a few things about the process.

A Bitcoin wallet is a secure account that shows you your transactions as well as stores your Bitcoin. A Bitcoin wallet is also called a Bitcoin client. When you open a Bitcoin wallet, you get a unique key - a public key and private key that is not similar to other people's keys. This key is what helps you trade your Bitcoin as well as send it to the people.

How the Bitcoin wallet works is that you generate a Bitcoin address anytime you plan to buy or get sent Bitcoin (BTC) from another person. You can also see the addresses in case that you want to submit BTCs to someone else. When a buyer and a seller agree to a transaction, they exchange the BTC, and other people can also see the trade because it is on the public network. In this system, you can look at the transactions but you cannot interact with other people's wallets other than your own.

Getting a Bitcoin Wallet

You can set up your wallet at Bitcoin.org. Here are the steps to follow and things to know.

1. **Tools of the trade**: If you want to know how you can get Bitcoin, you need Bitcoin software and a good internet connection. This is the first step for you to start using cryptocurrency. You can then begin opening your Bitcoin wallet.

2. **Inform yourself**: Ensure that you start being interested in Bitcoin. Everything in this book is enough to get you started. Another thing to note is that Bitcoin is a volatile currency that changes over time. It is not a great idea to put all your investments into Bitcoin. However, you can put a chunk of your money and see how it grows. One thing to note is that buying Bitcoin with PayPal or credit card is not easy. This is because you may be holding Bitcoin and you get a payment on PayPal and then the seller receives the payment. Such channels that are possible to reverse payments are not trustworthy because you may be transacting with someone you have never met. There is no way to ensure that you trust them. Equip yourself with such information.

3. **Choose your wallet**: This usually takes 10 to 15 minutes. Make sure you pick a Bitcoin system that you trust. They all work in the same way but the interfaces may be dissimilar. One of the main Bitcoin clients is *Multibit,* and this can be used in different operating systems. Bitcoin Wallet is also easy to use. If you do not want to install software on your computer, there is a solution. You can use a web-based wallet. However, experts do not recommend this because of security issues. There is no safety guarantee when it comes to the web-based platforms and you end up losing some of the control that you may have on computer-based

platforms. An example of an online wallet is *Coinbase*. You will also get a private key and an address on this one.

4. **Get Bitcoin**: One of the ways you can get this is to accept it as payment for goods and services. For example, if you provide some services online, someone can pay you with Bitcoin or another cryptocurrency. You can also convert another currency into Bitcoin. You can also buy Bitcoin through your local websites. A website like *localbitcoin.com* helps you see people in your area selling Bitcoin. You can see who gives you the best rate. For such transactions, you need to be very careful and do your research to avoid fraud. The best thing about this site is that people leave reviews for buyers and sellers and you can choose someone who is trustworthy. The second option is to use a Bitcoin Exchange. This is a site with a list of businesses that can help you Buy bitcoin through your banks. These may be a great option for beginners but remember that they are doing a service for you and you will have to pay them. It is better to learn the ropes and do it yourself because the information is readily available. It all depends on you and what you are willing to do. You can also use a Bitcoin ATM which works in the same way as a regular ATM. You can withdraw money so that you can purchase or sell Bitcoin. You can search for it to see the best one near you.

5. **Spend Bitcoin**: Now that more businesses are accepting Bitcoin as a form of payment, you can even use it to pay for your services.

One good example of a Bitcoin wallet is *Copay*. One way to keep your wallet safe is to enable a two-factor authentication system or store it offline. You will want to heighten your security as much as possible because there are people whose jobs are to look for ways to steal cryptocurrency.

Once you have a Bitcoin wallet, you can now trade Bitcoin through the different sites. Some of the most reputable ones are *Local Bitcoins, Coinbase, Spectrocoin* and *Kraken* (European).

This chapter has focused on having a Bitcoin wallet because it is the tool that enables you to carry out all the transactions. Without it, you cannot trade Bitcoin. Once you follow the steps outlined, you are now on your way to making some cash.

Chapter Four: Bitcoin Mining

You may have heard the term "Bitcoin Mining" floating around and you may be wondering what it is. This chapter will demystify what mining is and whether it is an excellent option for you.

Bitcoin Mining

Bitcoin Mining is a process where users on a network complete laborious mathematical computations using their computers. When the computer completes these calculations, the solution is verified by other users on the network and added to a public ledger called a *blockchain*. A blockchain is a system that contains all the transactions that occur. It is derived from the word block and chain. A block is a collection of different transactions, and many blocks make a chain. Both constitute the blockchain. In this blockchain, the first person who can solve the hard computation gets a payment and can claim the reward.

How It Works

Bitcoin mining is an expensive process but it is also gratifying. If you are interested in cryptocurrencies, this could be something that you can invest in. However, it is a very complicated process. You will need a computer that can handle the mining process.

BITCOIN

People are interested in mining because they get to create Bitcoin and they can sell it for some money. You do not have to be a Bitcoin miner to own virtual currency because you can just buy it using fiat money. However, mining is the way that all the Bitcoins came into existence, and the first Bitcoin was mined in 2009. People want to create their own money. It is similar to how the central bank mints cash but you are minting money in a controlled manner in a network.

You can mine Bitcoin in blocks which are units where you get rewards. A block has 12.5 Bitcoin as a reward. If you are solving these computations, you can earn Bitcoin in two ways. You can verify the different transactions that other users perform on the network and get paid, or you can be the first user to answer the mathematical equation and get paid. This process is called "proof of work."

You might be curious about what type of mathematical problems the miners are solving. They are trying to come up with a 64 decimal number called a hash. For example (22/7) can be divided into a 24 decimal system and the first person to solve that can earn a reward. The decimal system is a 64 hexadecimal system. This term means that the system has 64 digits which contain "0123456789" and "abcdef". An example of a 64 hexadecimal number is:

000000000000000000a4c4f4dad3dae6b54b3b678abe556 57f6789f43a371f6f

This number has 64 digits and includes both numbers and the first six letters of the alphabet.

However, you need a fast computer and a lot of computational power to reach such a figure and this why I said that mining is hard work. You need to have a high hash rate, which refers to how fast your computer can solve an equation. This power is measured through "megahashes," "gigahashes," or "terahashes" per second (MH/s, GH/s, and TH/s respectively). You can check the hash rates on the website *cryptocompare.com.*

Here is a good example of how this works. I tell you that I am thinking of a number between 1 and 5o. I tell you and other people to guess what number I am thinking of. If you are the first to shout the correct amount, you win and I reward you. If two people say the accurate numbers at the same time, I will pick the one who has done most work.

Think of this example but instead, assume that I am talking about a number between 1 and a million and I am asking millions of people to solve it. The system has millions of miners from all over the world and it knows how to ascertain who has won.

This is the same with the Bitcoin system. You and the other people trying to figure out the number I am thinking of are the miners. The reward I give the winner is the cryptocurrency. The system decides to honor the miner that has had the most transactions.

What You Need

If you need to mine, you will need a Graphics Processing Unit (GPU) and hardware like Antminer or ASIC miners. You also need some open source software and a Bitcoin wallet, which you learned how to set up in the previous chapter. However, be very wary and know that these wallets are prone to attack and there have been different heists and theft of Bitcoin. Once you lose them, there will be no way to get them back. These are very expensive hence why people do not opt to mine solo. However, with some cryptocurrency like Etherium, people can mine by themselves because they can buy low-cost graphics cards to begin.

The software to use can be GUIminer, which you can install on your computer. When you install it, you can start to mine instantly. The more powerful a machine is, the better it is at mining.

Back in the day, an average computer would be able to generate Bitcoin and it was effortless for people to mine. This process became harder as more Bitcoins were created. There is also new hardware being produced that is specially made to perform this task. An example is the ASIC (Application Specific Integrated Circuit). You can also buy a mining rig but it is costly at around $12,000. This is a lot of money to invest and I would not advise you to buy it.

Another thing is that you need a lot of electricity to mine because the computer consumes a lot of power. When you are making your calculations on whether Bitcoin mining is a profitable venture, remember to factor in electricity as one of the costs.

You also need to monitor the price of Bitcoin regularly. Bookmark different sites. Learn more about other cryptocurrencies so that when things are on the downward spiral, you can convert your Bitcoin to another more favorable option and diversify your options.

Mining Pools

Mining pools are collections of people who mine Bitcoin by putting their computers and power together to reap the benefits. All the users then receive a percentage of the Bitcoin reward. Websites like *Slush's Pool* help small miners come together. You get a percentage depending on your computing power so the stronger your computer is, the more money you get. With such a system, you can get a few dollars daily. However, this method is not regulated and there is no guarantee that the pool operator has to give you the Bitcoin.

Note that Bitcoin mining is not the best of options especially for a beginner. If you do not have a reliable computer, there is no need to break your back investing your money to buy the computer and hardware. You are better off buying Bitcoin and trading it. This approach will help you steer clear of unwanted losses.

This chapter has looked at mining Bitcoin and everything you need to know. You have also seen your options which are solo mining and pool mining. Whichever you choose, remember that there are companies that have dedicated their computing power to mine Bitcoin and you are competing with them. Do not have high expectations of making it big if you do not have such resources. You must also have the patience. You are now better placed to decide if this is the direction you want to take.

Chapter Five:
Making Money from Bitcoin

This chapter will look at how you can make money from Bitcoin and all the options you have. Over the last few months, Bitcoin's value has skyrocketed, and more businesses are coming on board to accept Bitcoin as a form of payment.

Making Money

There are many options when it comes to making money with Bitcoin. Some of these methods will earn you small amounts of money but others will give you a considerable amount. You can combine some to get multiple sources of income.

Here are some ways how you can make money with Bitcoin:

1. **Solo mining**: We have looked at mining in the previous chapter. If you decide that this is the way to go, you may make some money that way.

2. **Join a mining pool**: You can also join other small miners and combine your computing power. We have touched on this in the previous chapter.

3. **Faucets**: There are simple tasks that you can perform on websites and get paid in Bitcoin. For example, you can solve captcha codes and get some money in your Bitcoin Wallet. These websites make cash through ads and they need

traffic. You are part of the traffic and when you solve captchas, they get some money from Google or any other web operators. These faucets take a lot of time and energy from you because you are always solving different puzzles. They can be tiring but if you are up for it, it can be a way to make that extra cash. It takes a while to get a considerable amount of Bitcoin.

4. **Phone games**: One mobile game that pays people with cryptocurrency is *crypto android space*. Sometimes the players in the game can also view advertisements and they get a small amount of Bitcoin. People earn more money by referring their friends to join the site.

5. **Paidbooks**: *Paidbook.com* is a site that pays people some money for reading books. It works in the same way as the captcha codes but people just read a book and they get paid. It pays people in Satoshi (cryptocurrency).

6. **Watching videos**: You can also earn Bitcoin by watching some videos on sites like *Vidybit*. Your Satoshi payments have to accrue to a certain amount before you can withdraw them.

7. **Trading Bitcoin**: Trading is one of the most recommended methods of making money. The trick with this option is to buy low and sell high. The best thing is that you do not have to buy a whole Bitcoin. You can actually start with what you have, and over time, the money will appreciate. However, there have been instances of hackers attacking platforms where people hold cash, so know that it is not 100% secure. An example of a website that was hacked is *Bitfinex*.

The trading process requires patience and monitoring of different sites and news. Keep your ear on the ground so that you know what is happening with the price of Bitcoin to ensure that you are not doing this blindly.

Way Forward

So what is the way forward for you? It is up to you to tap into the value of Bitcoin. You need to recognize that the growth is swift. People who invested their money in October 2017 have doubled their investments. What makes it appreciate in value is the fact the demand is rising so fast as more people start to know about it.

Be very cautious because anything can happen. As we mentioned, one of the disadvantages of this cryptocurrency is that it is very unpredictable. If too many people hold it, it devalues. If too many people release it, it also affects the value negatively. Ensure that you diversify your portfolio. Do not store all your money in Bitcoin. Invest money that you consider to be a surplus in case things go wrong. On the other hand, remember that this risk could very quickly pay off.

Ensure that you always have the latest information. Nowadays, many reputable websites give the newest development in Bitcoin. Another strategy is to go to the Google search bar and to search Bitcoin then click on the news tab. Look at valuable resources like the *New York Times* and *Fortune Magazine*. Compare the prices and have a love for numbers because some of this data is presented in figures. You should also learn how to read the charts. Acquiring such kind of knowledge will inform your decision on when to buy or sell.

Take great care of your online wallet. Ensure that your private key is safe. It does not hurt to be extra careful. Enable two-factor authentication. Sign out of any computer that you use. Store your passwords secretly. Use websites that you trust. Do your research before using any website for transactions.

Overall, as you enjoy your Bitcoin journey, take every necessary step to secure your money.

Conclusion

In conclusion, after reading this book, you now have a better understanding of Bitcoin. A lot of thought went into its development and it is a very complex but groundbreaking technology. It is a miracle that it has grown to such a magnitude.

There are rapid developments with this technology that crop up every day and facilitate the use of this currency. As the world economy changes, we can predict that Bitcoin will be a prime payment option.

We have explored how the cryptocurrency works and how it is generated. We have looked at setting up your wallet and bitcoin mining. However, ensure that you ponder over whether you want to be involved or not. If you decide to become involved, set up a Bitcoin client/wallet and you will join the network. Purchase or trade bitcoin and start on your journey. As mentioned, Bitcoin mining is not advisable at this point especially if you plan to do it alone. However, it is not impossible if you have the computing power at your disposal. You also need to do your research.

This book has given you the basics of Bitcoin and this information will help you get into this venture. However, there are always developments on Bitcoin cryptocurrency. You can compare the price of Bitcoin at *coindesk.com/price/* or on *charts.bitcoin.com*. These sites will help you monitor the amount even before investing and after investing. You will know when to cash out or when to hold the bitcoin.

Share the news with your friends and family and spread the word. The more people know about them the better. Educate people and let them know if this is for them. You can even refer them to this book.

You have all the information that you need from this book. If a particular chapter or point was not clear, go back to it until you have understood it. With this information, you are well on your way to making a substantial fortune!

Resources

https://www.investopedia.com/terms/b/bitcoin-mining.asp

https://www.amazon.in/Beginners-Guide-Bitcoin-Cryptocurrencies-ebook/dp/B072F48NFG

https://www.cnbc.com/2014/01/23/cnbc-explains-how-to-mine-bitcoins-on-your-own.html

https://www.cryptocoinsnews.com/earn-money-bitcoin-%E2%80%8B/

https://www.bitcoinmining.com/getting-started/

https://99bitcoins.com/how-to-make-money-with-bitcoin/

https://www.coindesk.com/bitcoin-explained-five-year-old/

http://www.techradar.com/news/software/business-software/understanding-bitcoin-and-crypto-currency-1240479

Thank you for reading this book and please leave at honest review at

https://www.amazon.com/dp/B078L85GTQ

Thank you!
Charlie Pryce

www.ingramcontent.com/pod-product-compliance
Lightning Source LLC
Chambersburg PA
CBHW030103230526
45471CB00003B/1225